Kinesthetic Vocabulary Activities Your Child Will Love:

In Just 27 Days Improve Your Kinesthetic Child's Vocabulary and Reading Comprehension

By Ricki Linksman

National Reading Diagnostics Institute

  ISBN: 978-1-928997-17-7

Kinesthetic Vocabulary Activities Your Child Will Love:

In Just 27 Days Improve Your Kinesthetic Child's Vocabulary and Reading Comprehension

by Ricki Linksman

Published by: National Reading Diagnostics Institute
                       Naperville, IL 60563

First printing: 1993
Revised edition: 2012

ISBN: 978-1-928997-17-7

Printed in the United States of America

Other Books, Audio, Programs, E-Courses, & Coaching by Ricki Linksman

The Fine Line between ADHD and Kinesthetic Learners: 197 Kinesthetic Activities to Quickly Improve Reading, Memory and Learning: The Ultimate Parent Handbook for ADHD, ADD, and Kinesthetic Learners by Ricki Linksman (To order, visit: **www.keystolearningsuccess.com**)

Off the Wall Phonics: For Kids on the Move): Kinesthetic Phonics Games: (10 Award-winning Game levels of 10 games each to accelerate reading. Prove to raise reading levels in 98% of all students (grades K-12) by accelerating them from 3-5 grade levels through these 10 game levels. (To order, visit **www.keystolearningsuccess.com or www.keyslearning.com**

Keys to Reading Success™: An online Internet based pre-K-12 and College accelerated brain-based reading program, with reading diagnostic tests, phonics diagnostic tests that parents or teachers can use and a Superlinks assessment to find students' fastest way of learning, including learning style and brain hemispheric preference; an individual prescriptive plan on improving reading, and thousands of lesson plans and fun activities from pre-K-12, and college in all components of reading (comprehension, phonics, fluency, vocabulary, test-taking skills, memory, and phonemic awareness) in all learning styles (visual, auditory, tactile, and kinesthetic) (The phonics test and Superlinks test is available in Spanish also.) Visit: www.keystoreadingsuccess.com

Superlinks to Accelerated Learning™: An online Internet brain-based assessment to find one's fastest way of learning, including learning style and brain hemispheric preference; and a detailed individual report with strategies on best way to learn, best materials to use, and best way to communicate (pre-K, K-12, college and adult) (Spanish version is also available). Visit: **www.superlinkslearning.com**

For other product, books, audios, coaching, and summer or after-school courses produced by Ricki Linksman visit any of the following:
www.readinginstruction.com
www.keystolearningsuccess.com
www.keyslearning.com
www.keystoreadingsuccess.com   **www.superlinkslearning.com**

Kinesthetic Vocabulary Activities Your Child Will Love

In Just 27 Days Improve Your Kinesthetic Child's Vocabulary and Reading Comprehension

by Ricki Linksman

Table of Contents

Kinesthetic Vocabulary Activities Your Child Will Love

Introduction

By Ricki Linksman

Kinesthetic Vocabulary Activities Your Child Will Love: In Just 30 Days Improve Your Kinesthetic Child's Vocabulary and Reading Comprehension offers to parents vocabulary strategies to improve vocabulary and reading comprehension for kinesthetic learners quickly. Kinesthetic learners learn best through movement of their body and muscles. These kinesthetic vocabulary activities are fun and engaging. They will boost a kinesthetic learner's memory so he or she can master a large amount of new vocabulary words quickly. If you do one kinesthetic vocabulary activity from this book a day, your kinesthetic child's vocabulary and reading comprehension will grow in 27 days!

This book will teach your child the vocabulary strategy of HOW TO learn new words. By teaching your kinesthetic child these kinesthetic strategies to learn ANY new vocabulary word quickly you empower your child to build his or her own vocabulary for life! Once kinesthetic children learn the basic kinesthetic strategies for attacking new words, they can repeat the technique with any new words they encounter.

There are three main techniques for getting the meaning of new words. The first is looking up the definition in a dictionary or glossary, a skill that every child needs to learn. The second approach is getting the meaning of the word from the context, which means using clues in the sentence or passage to figure out what the unknown word means. There are a variety of context-clue skills you can teach your child. The third is using knowledge of word parts—roots, prefixes, and suffixes— to figure out what the word means.

In this book you will get one fun kinesthetic activity and strategy a day so that in 27 days you can teach your kinesthetic child how to learn new vocabulary words quickly and improve kinesthetic reading comprehension dramatically. Have fun with your kinesthetic child in your journey into these enjoyable kinesthetic vocabulary activities.

Part 1:

Kinesthetic

Dictionary

Skills

Chapter 1
Day 1

Teaching Your Kinesthetic Child
How to Use a Dictionary or Glossary

If your kinesthetic child is in first through third grades, you will need a beginner's dictionary. If your kinesthetic child is in fourth through sixth grades, you will need an intermediate dictionary. If your kinesthetic child or teen is in middle school or high school, you can use any standard dictionary.

Allow your child to stand up or move around for the following activity. As you explain and point, have the child follow-up by pointing what you pointed to, while standing up or being stretched out comfortably. Begin by pointing out how a dictionary is set up. Explain that the words are arranged alphabetically. If your child is in first, second, or third grade, he or she may not understand what alphabetical order is. You will have to explain that the words are listed in the order that letters appear in the alphabet. Take large 8 ½ x 11 construction paper, and select six words from the dictionary. Have the child copy one word per sheet to make large size word cards. Do this with 6 different words. Then, have the child lay the 6 words on the carpet in alphabetical order. You can model it first, showing how alphabetical order works and then mix up the cards and have your child attempt it again and again until he or she understands the concept.

Point out the guidewords on the top of each page of the dictionary. Show your child that if you are looking up a word that starts with h, you have to flip through the book until you come to the h words.

Explain that the first guideword shows which word is at the beginning of the page. The second guideword shows which word is at the end of the page. All the words on the page will be in between the two guidewords.

You and your child can make a giant poster of the sample words below on a model of a dictionary page, with the guidewords written large on the top of the page, and the rest of the words listed below it. This will help your child get a kinesthetic experience of how guidewords work.

You must point out that there are many words that begin with h. After finding h, we must look at the second letter in the word. If the word is hippopotamus, we must then look up the guidewords that have hi. After locating the hi words, we must look at the third letter, which is p. We must then look up guidewords that have hip. If hip is not a guide word, we must look at the letter before p, such as hio and then hin, and after p, such as hiq, then hir, then his. When we find the guidewords for hip words, we then know to look on that page. The entry words are written in darker black, or bold ink. We skim down the list of bold words looking for hip. When we get to hip, then we look at the fourth letter, which is p. We then begin looking for hipp. We continue to compare each letter of the word we want with the entry words until we find our word. For example:

hint	history
hint	his
hip	Hispanic
hipbone	hiss
hippopotamus	history

Next, you will need to teach your child what to do after finding the entry word. Model physically while explaining that the definition of the word is written. Help your child make a giant poster, with your child doing the writing, of the word with its definition. There may be several definitions. The child will have to try each definition and see which fits the meaning of the rest of the sentence. To begin with, read the sentence, thinking of the word as meaning number 1. Ask your child, "Does this make sense?" If not, read the sentence, thinking of the word as meaning number 2. Again ask your child, "Does this meaning make sense?" If not, continue reading the word in the sentence, thinking about each of the meanings, until you find the one that makes sense.

Point out that the dictionary also gives the part of speech. Help your child make a giant poster of the dictionary word with its part of speech. This will be meaningful to children in grades four and up. They should be able to determine whether the word is a noun, verb, adjective, or adverb. Help your kinesthetic child make large index cards, with one card saying "noun," another saying "verb," etc. Your child can tape the correct colored card with the right part of speech next to the word and its definition of the giant poster made. Use different colored index cards for each part of speech. In some dictionaries, the word is used in a sentence as an example. Point this out to the child. If the dictionary also gives synonyms or opposites, you can point that out as well. Help your child make a different colored index card saying, "Synonyms," and one with a different color saying, "Antonyms." Have your child stick the correct index card on the giant poster of the word with its definition, wherever the dictionary listing identifies either the synonym or antonym. Pre-select words to put on the poster that has either a synonym or antonym so your child can experience identifying that entry by sticking the colored index card on it.

Kinesthetic Sports Move Bonus:

For each task, correctly performed, give your child or teen one award point, followed by a sports move for another bonus point. The sports move can be throwing a ball into a basketball hoop, throwing or kicking a football toward a goal, putting a golf ball into a hole, kicking a soccer ball to a goal, or any other sports move your child or teen likes. Keep track of the points, and make an award chart showing prizes can be earned for different amounts of points. There can be small and large size prizes. Kinesthetic learners love to win!

Chapter 2:
Day 2

Kinesthetic Vocabulary Record-Keeping

You will want your kinesthetic child to begin some kind of record keeping for the new words he or she looks up in a dictionary. After looking up the word once, chances are that your child will forget the meaning. It is important for your child to write the word and its meaning using his or her kinesthetic large muscles and do some activities with the word that will help him or her remember its meaning. It is said that a person must use a word at least seven times to own it. If your child does this kinesthetically he or she can remember it in less tries, and often even in one try! The following lessons include some ways your child can keep a record of new words, followed by activities to help your child remember the new word.

Kinesthetic Sports Move Bonus:

As your child or teen remembers each new word, give him or her one award point, followed by a sports move for another bonus point. The sports move can be throwing a ball into a basketball hoop, throwing or kicking a football toward a goal, putting a golf ball into a hole, kicking a soccer ball to a goal, or any other sports move your child or teen likes. Keep track of the points, and make an award chart showing prizes can be earned for different amounts of points. There can be small and large size prizes.

Chapter 3:
Day 3

Kinesthetic Vocabulary Mind-Mapping

After looking up the word, have your kinesthetic child act out a situation in which the word could be used. Have your child draw a cartoon action story in which the word is used, and have your child write the word in a bubble.

Help your kinesthetic child make a mind map in which the new vocabulary word is written into a middle bubble or circle on large flip chart paper. Have bubbles or circles shooting off the main word. In one bubble, have your child write the definition and draw a picture to show an action that goes with the word. In another bubble, write the part of speech and in another write a synonym for the word. In another bubble write an antonym, or opposite. In a large bubble, have your child write a sentence using that word and draw an illustration that goes with it.

Chapter 4

Day 4

Helping Your Kinesthetic Child

Remember New Vocabulary Words

The key to keeping information in long-term kinesthetic memory is attaching it to an action. You must take the word and think of it in as a movement of the large muscles or action. The situation has to be as far-out and as outrageous as you can make it. Your kinesthetic child can either write the situation on large flip chart paper while standing up, while reading it aloud, acting it out, or drawing a large-size picture of it. The more humorous, action-packed, or even ridiculous his or her example, the more likely your kinesthetic child will be to remember the word and its meaning.

Here are some examples:

Example 1:

    taciturn: quiet

Have your child act out a dog named Taci taking a turn, and then sitting quietly. Then have your child stand up to write the word taciturn and draw a cartoon of a dog on large-size paper or flip chart paper, while saying aloud, "Taci, you dog, turn around and be quiet."

Example 2:

bifurcated: split into two

Explain to your child that bi means "two," as in bicycle, or "two wheels," or bimonthly, meaning "every two months." Then have your child act out and then write the word and draw a large-size picture, while standing up, of a giant fork in the road that is split. One prong of the fork points to one road, and the other prong in the fork points to another road. Say, "Bifurcated is a 'fork' which is split into 'bi' or "two." Have your child draw a giant fork, split into two parts, and say, "Bifurcated."

Try to find words your child knows that sound like the new word, and then have your child act it out, write it, and draw a picture of it while standing up. This will help bring back the word and meaning to your child's mind more easily.

Chapter 5
Day 5

Kinesthetic Vocabulary Charades

Help your child make a list of words and their definitions. Take turns with your kinesthetic child selecting a word and acting it out silently, so the other can guess which word is being dramatized. If you go first, select a word, act it out, and have your child guess which word you are acting out. Then have your child select a word and act it out, and you guess the meaning. Points can be awarded for each correct guess.

Notes of Words Your Want to Use:

Chapter 6
Day 6

Kinesthetic Vocabulary Search

Award your kinesthetic child or teen a point each time he or she uses a new vocabulary word correctly throughout the day. Have him or her act it out as well. Have your child or teen search for opportunities to use the new word. Each time you catch him or her using the new vocabulary word correctly, give him or her one point. Determine the number of points needed to win a prize.

Each time your child or teen finds a new word and uses it, add a bonus reward by having him or her do a sports move, like throw a ball into a basketball hoop, throw or kick a football or soccer ball toward a goal, putt a golf ball into a hole, do ring toss, or any other activity your child or teen likes.

Notes of Words You Want to Use:

Chapter 7
Day 7

Kinesthetic Dictionary Cross-Country

Give your kinesthetic child practice in looking up words in a dictionary. Provide your child with a list of ten new words selected from a current book your child is reading.

Use a stopwatch to see how quickly your child or teen looks up each word. Chart the results.

Each day, give your child or teen ten new words and see if your child can beat his or her own record.

Add rewards of a point for each word your child or teen looks up correctly. Each time that he or she finds a new word and uses it, add a bonus reward by having him or her do a sports move, like throw a ball into a basketball hoop, throw or kick a football or soccer ball into a goal, putt a golf ball into a hole, do ring toss, or any other sports move your child or teen enjoys.

Chapter 8

Day 8

Kinesthetic Alphabetical Card Sort

Help your kinesthetic child write a list of words on large 8 ½ x 11 inch colored construction paper, one word per page. Mix them up. Have your child arrange the cards in alphabetical order. This will provide practice for looking up words in alphabetical order in a dictionary or glossary.

Part 2:

Kinesthetic

Context Clues

Chapter 9
Day 9

Teaching Your Kinesthetic Child
about Context Clues

Using context clues to derive word meaning is one of the skills taught in schools. It is like detective work. One must figure out the meaning of the new word by using clues provided in the rest of the sentence.

Here is an example:

John was elated when he won the race.

Suppose your child did not know the meaning of the word elated. To figure out its meaning from the context, you would ask your kinesthetic child to act out the sentence, and then ask him or her, "How do you think John felt when he won the race?"

Your child may say, "Happy."

Then you would say, "That's correct. So elated must mean something like 'feeling happy.'" To confirm the meaning, have your child look it up in the dictionary.

Why would one want to use context clues in place of using a dictionary? Often, when reading for pleasure, or when time is short, one does not have the time to look up the word. Thus, one could figure out what the word might mean by using the context without breaking the reading to find a dictionary. Ideally, students should keep a list of new words and the page they find them on, and look them up at some point in order to expand their vocabulary. However, if this is not possible due to a time constraint, students can use context clues.

There are various types of context clues one can use. In one case, the new word is given and its meaning is also provided in the sentence:

Example:

On a nature walk, Jill saw a heron, a type of bird.

In this case, the new word, heron, is defined as "a type of bird." In many textbooks the new word is often defined in the same sentence.

Another type of context clue gives the opposite meaning:

Example:

Unlike easygoing, agreeable Sally, Pat was obstinate.

From this sentence, one gets a clue that obstinate must be the opposite of easygoing and agreeable.

A third type of context clue gives the meaning through information provided in the entire passage.

Example:

Bill had worked hard to try out for the baseball team. His older brother, Tom, kept telling him he would not make it. Tom's friends even made fun of Bill. Bill wanted to try out anyway. On the day of the tryouts, Tom and his friends were there to watch. Bill tried his best, but missed the ball every time. Tom and his friends would laugh. Every time Bill missed the ball, Bill felt so chagrined he wanted to hide.

To determine the meaning of chagrined, the reader would have to figure out how they would feel in Bill's place. Some would say they felt embarrassed or humiliated, which is the correct meaning. Using context clues is not as accurate as looking the word up in a dictionary, but one can come fairly close. In the above example, some students may say that Bill felt frustrated or angry, which is not the correct meaning. There is room for error in the context-clue method. However, one would have the clue that Bill was not happy about the situation and was not feeling good.

Chapter 10

Day 10

How to Use Context Clues with
Your Kinesthetic Child

Go over the three types of context clues given in the examples above with your kinesthetic child. Then take one of your child's books and locate some words that your child does not know. Science and social studies textbooks are filled with examples in which new vocabulary can be figured out using context clues. Guide your child to find the words' meanings by using the context clues. Have your child decide which type of context clues is given. Is the meaning given in the sentence? Is the opposite meaning given? Alternatively, does one have to figure out the meaning from the situation in the sentence or paragraph? Have your child identify which type of context clue is used.

Kinesthetic Context Clues Sports Move Bonus:

For each task, correctly performed, give your child or teen one award point, followed by a sports move for another bonus point. The sports move can be throwing a ball into a basketball hoop, throwing or kicking a football toward a goal, putting a golf ball into a hole, kicking a soccer ball to a goal, or any other sports move your child or teen likes. Keep track of the points, and make an award chart showing prizes can be earned for different amounts of points.

Chapter 11

Day 11

Kinesthetic Context Clue Search

Make a large poster size chart with three headings:

Definition Given in the Sentence or Passage	Opposite Meaning Given in the Sentence or Passage	Clues Given in the Situation Described in the Passage

Search in books for new words, and have your child identify which of the three types of context clues is used. List the words under the appropriate heading on the chart. Have your child find out which type of clue they find more of in their books.

Kinesthetic Sports Move Bonus:

For each word found, give your child or teen one award point, followed by a sports move for another bonus point. The sports move can be throwing a ball into a basketball hoop, throwing or kicking a football toward a goal, putting a golf ball into a hole, kicking a soccer ball to a goal, or any other sports move your child or teen likes. Keep track of the points, and make an award chart showing prizes can be earned for different amounts of points.

Chapter 12

Day 12

Kinesthetic Context Clue Olympics

As you read with your kinesthetic child, allowing for standing up, stretching out and freedom of movement of the muscles, have your child identify new words he or she does not know. First, have your child figure out the meaning using the context clues. Then have your child look up the word in the dictionary. See if your child's definition matches the dictionary's meaning.

For every time the definition your child figured out from the context clues was the correct one according to the dictionary, award him or her one point. Determine the number of points your child needs for a reward. The reward could be going out to your child's favorite restaurant, buying your child a new book, or going to a place of amusement your child enjoys. Sometimes when the task is difficult, like spending time on vocabulary building, including a reward makes it more like a game for the child.

Bonus Sports Moves:

Add a bonus point for throwing the ball in a basketball hoop, or kicking a football or soccer ball into a goal (if outdoors), or any game task as a bonus reward for extra points for correct definitions.

Part 3:

Using Word Parts to Help

Your Kinesthetic Child

Get the Meaning of Words

Chapter 13

Day 13

Helping Your Kinesthetic Child Use Word Parts to Get the Meaning of Words

A third method of figuring out the meaning of a new word is using word parts. Some words are made up of two parts: a root word and a prefix, or a root word and a suffix. There are some words that have a root, a prefix, and a suffix. In the following subsections, you will learn what these words mean.

Kinesthetic Word Parts Sports Move Bonus:

For each task, correctly performed, give your child or teen one award point, followed by a sports move for another bonus point. The sports move can be throwing a ball into a basketball hoop, throwing or kicking a football toward a goal, putting a golf ball into a hole, kicking a soccer ball to a goal, or any other sports move your child or teen likes. Keep track of the points, and make an award chart showing prizes can be earned for different amounts of points. There can be small and large size prizes. Kinesthetic learners love to compete and win!

Chapter 14

Day 14

How Knowledge of Prefixes Helps to
Derive Word Meaning

A prefix is a group of letters added to the beginning of a word. The prefix gives the word a new meaning. Some prefixes are re-, de-, pre-, un-, dis-, con-, etc.

For example, re means "to do over" or "do again."

When re is added to the word write, we get rewrite, which means "to write again." When re is added to the word do, we get redo, which means "to do again." By knowing the meaning of the prefix re, the child can figure out many words:

redraw

revisit

regain

retry

remake

Here is another example. Pre means "before." When pre is added to the word test, we get pretest, or "to test beforehand." We know that a pretest is a test the child receives before the actual test. When pre is added to the word view, we get preview, or "to view or see before." In a preview of a movie, we see the movie before it comes out to the general public. If the child knows that pre means "before," the child can figure out the meaning of many words that start with pre:

preassign

predate

prepay

Other prefix definitions are:

dis: not

un: not

con: against

ir: not

be: to be

non: not

uni: one

bi: two

tri: three

quad: four

quin: five

sex: six

sept: seven

oct: eight

nov: nine

deca: ten

cent: hundred

milli: thousand

semi: half

hemi: half

Kinesthetic Sports Move Bonus:

Remember to award a point and bonus sports move for each task, correctly performed, towards prizes!

Chapter 15

Day 15

Kinesthetic Prefix Word Search

Help your child make a chart listing prefixes. Make the chart large size on flip chart paper so your kinesthetic child can work on it while standing up, or stretched out on the floor.

Have your child find as many words as possible that begin with those prefixes and write them in columns. This can be done two ways.

1) The child can search for words starting with those prefixes in

his or her books; or

2) The child can look up those prefixes in the dictionary and list

the words he or she finds.

Have your child act out the word. Then, on the flip chart paper, next to each word, have your child write the definition of the word using the prefix meaning and draw an action picture. For example:

bimonthly: two times a month

hemisphere: half a sphere

dissatisfied: not satisfied

You can use the prefixes from Chapter 13 as a starting point.

Bonus Sports Move:

For every word your kinesthetic child finds, award a point. For every point, give a bonus chance to do a physical activity, like putting a golf ball into a hole, kicking or throwing a football to a goal, kicking a soccer ball towards a goal, throwing a ring on a pole for ring toss, throwing a ball into a basketball hoop, or any other fun activity.

Chapter 16

Day 16

Kinesthetic Prefix Clues

While reading with your kinesthetic child, point out some of the words that begin with a prefix. Have your child look up the meaning of the prefix and figure out what the word means using the prefix meaning. For example:

Lilly had to rewrite her lesson.

Your child will look up re and find that it means "to do again." Your child should figure out that rewrite means "to write again."

Have your child act out each word found. Then, have your child write the word and the definition on large flip chart paper or a white board.

Bonus Sports Move:

For every word your kinesthetic child finds, award a point. For every point, give a bonus chance to do a physical activity, like throwing a ring on a pole for ring toss, throwing or kicking a football or soccer ball toward a goal, or throwing a ball into a basketball hoop.

Chapter 17
Day 17

How Knowledge of Suffixes Helps to Derive Word Meaning

A suffix is a group of letters attached to the end of a word. The suffix gives the word a new meaning. Some suffix endings are -able, -/u/, -i/y, -ness, -/ess.

For example: the suffix -ful means "full of." If ful is added to the word beauty, we get beautiful, or "full of beauty." If -ful is added to the word sorrow, we get sorrowful, or "full of sorrow."

The suffix- less means "not having" or "having less." Thus, penniless means "not having a penny."

The suffix -able means "able to." Thus, lovable means "able to be loved." Livable means "able to be lived in."

Bonus Sports Move:

Remember to award a point for the task done correctly, and a bonus sports move for more points!

Chapter 18

Day 18

Kinesthetic Suffix Search

Help your kinesthetic child list a variety of suffixes on a chart. Make the chart with large size paper so your child can stand up while making it or stretch out on the floor.

Have your kinesthetic child search for words in his or her books that end in those suffixes and list them on the chart. Next to each word, have your child write the definition, using the suffix meaning.

For example:

excusable: able to be excused

Have your child act out the meaning of the word.

Your child can also illustrate the word with large action type sketches on the large flip chart paper.

Bonus Sports Move:

For every word found, award a point to your kinesthetic child, leading to a predetermined prize for a certain number of points. Add a physical activity as a bonus reward for extra points for each word found.

Chapter 19
Day 19

Kinesthetic Suffix Race

Using the suffix list created in Chapter 18, have your kinesthetic child see how many words he or she can find that uses each of the suffix. You can set a timer for five minutes to see how many words he or she finds in that amount of time.

After finding the words, your kinesthetic child should post them on a flip chart or white board and write the definition, in large size while standing up. Track the number of words found within five minutes as a score. Then, see if your child can beat his or her own record by finding more words in less time.

Chapter 20

Day 20

Kinesthetic Suffix Board Game

Help your kinesthetic child make a large size game board in which a word with a suffix is written in each space on the game board. Each space can be a large sheet of 8 ½ by 11 inch colored construction paper or poster board.

The theme of the game can be a car race, space race, boat race, motorcycle race, or anything in which your child is interested. The game can be played by throwing the dice and moving a game piece around the board. The game can also be played with your child moving around the large spaces.

The player must correctly read the word on the space in order to stay on the spot. Otherwise, the player must return to his or her previous position. The first player to cross the finish line wins.

Chapter 21

Day 21

How Knowledge of Roots

Helps to Derive Word Meaning

A root word is the base word upon which prefixes and suffixes are added. Many of the words in the English language are derived from other languages, such as Latin or Greek. Knowledge of the original Latin or Greek can give clues to word meaning.

For example, if one knows that the Greek word part -ology means "study of" and bio means "life," we will know that biology means "the study of life."

If we know that geo- refers to the earth, we will know that geology is the study of the earth.

If we know that zoo means "animals," then zoology is the study of animals.

If we know that optic refers to the eye, then we can have a good idea of the meaning of optometrist, ophthalmologist, and optician, as those who work with the eye.

Chapter 22

Day 22

Kinesthetic Root Word Search

Give your kinesthetic child the following root words and see how many words he or she can find in his or her books or in a dictionary that use that root:

ped:	foot
scope:	to see
cardio:	heart
graph:	to write
cycle:	wheel
astro:	space
mobile:	moving
aqua:	water
tele:	far
geo:	earth
phone:	sound
marine:	water
vision:	to see

Examples: telephone, television, telecommunications, telegraph

Have your kinesthetic child write the word and its definition on large flip chart paper while standing up or stretched out on the floor.

Next to each word, ask your kinesthetic child to write the definitions. For example:

telephone: sound from far away

television: to see from far away

Your child can act out the word, and also add a large, quick action sketch next to the written word on the flip chart.

Bonus Sports Move:

Reward your child with bonus points for each word found and allow for a physical sport activity for a bonus point.

Chapter 23

Day 23

Kinesthetic Invent-a-Word

Have your kinesthetic child combine roots, prefixes, and suffixes to invent new words and write the meanings of each.

For example:

aquascope: a machine to see water

astrocycle: a bicycle to ride in space.

Have your child write the word on large flip chart paper while standing up or stretched out on the floor.

Have your child to act out the word. Your child can also draw a large size quick action picture of the newly invented words next to the meaning.

Chapter 24
Day 24

Kinesthetic Magazine Search

Have your child search through a magazine to look for root words he or she knows and circle them with a colored magic marker or pen. Then have your child write the word on large flip chart paper while standing up or stretched out on the floor.

Have your child figure out the meaning of the words using the knowledge of the root's meaning. Then, have your child act out the words found, or draw a large action picture on the flip chart paper next to the word.

Chapter 25

Day 25

Kinesthetic Object Search

Have your child search to find objects in the house or yard whose name contains a root word.

Have your child write the word and its meaning on large 8 ½ by 11 inch colored construction paper and tape it to the object.

Example:

> telescope
> bicycle
> television

Kinesthetic Sports Move Bonus:

Remember to award a point and bonus sports move for each task, correctly performed, towards prizes!

Part 4:

Combining All the

Kinesthetic Vocabulary Skills

Chapter 26

Day 26

Pulling All the Vocabulary Skills Together

After going through the different methods one can use to figure out the meaning of new words, review them with your kinesthetic child.

Ask your child to tell you what he or she can do to figure out the meaning of a new word. Your child should be able to tell you the three following techniques:

- look it up in a dictionary or glossary
- use the context clues
- use knowledge of prefixes, suffixes, or roots

As you read with your child and he or she gets stumped by a new word, instead of telling your child what to do, ask, "What technique can you use to figure out the word?" It is important that your child remember the strategies, because you will not always be with your child when he or she reads, such as when he or she is in school. Your child needs to know the strategies in order to read and learn independently.

If your child still cannot repeat to you any of the three strategies listed above, repeat the lessons given in this book for those techniques that he or she forgot. The time you spend on these vocabulary activities will be time well spent, for your child will need these skills for his or her entire school career and later in life.

Kinesthetic Sports Move Bonus:

Award a point and bonus sports move for each task, correctly performed, towards prizes!

Chapter 27

Day 27

Keep a Personal Kinesthetic Dictionary

As your kinesthetic child looks up new words, help him or her start a personal kinesthetic dictionary. You can use large flip chart paper or poster board for your child to make his or her own book. You can punch holes in the sides and use string to bind the book together.

Your child may wish to list new words alphabetically or by category. Your child can also illustrate with large size, quick action sketches.

He or she may wish to list words by part of speech, such as nouns, verbs, adverbs, or adjectives, or your child may wish to list them according to categories such as sports, medicine, foods, animals, etc. Periodically review with your child the words in the dictionary to reinforce them. Remember, words must be used about seven times in order for them to become part of one's memory.

Kinesthetic Sports Move Bonus:

Also track all the award points earned for each task, correctly performed, towards prizes!

Part 5

Kinesthetic Vocabulary for High School Students

Chapter 28

Vocabulary for Kinesthetic High School Students: Preparing for College Entrance Tests

If your kinesthetic child is a teen in high school, he or she may want to prepare for college entrance tests. On the SAT, one portion of the test involves vocabulary. On the ACT, vocabulary knowledge is needed to understand the reading comprehension stories and texts, and answer vocabulary questions about the meaning of words used in the text.

There are books on the market containing word lists of important words frequently used on college entrance exams. Learning those words on those lists can help your child study for these tests. These preparatory books contain lists of words. In studying word lists, use the kinesthetic vocabulary techniques described in Parts 1 through 4 of this book to help your kinesthetic child memorize the words. Teach your child to connect each word with an action in order to memorize the meanings.

Many of the words in the lists are built from roots, suffixes, and prefixes your kinesthetic child can learn. The techniques in this book can help your child study these lists in preparation for the college exams.

Bonus Sports Move: For each task performed correctly award 1 point and a bonus point for each successful sports move, whether basketball, golf, football, or soccer. These can add up to prizes your teen would enjoy winning.

Chapter 29

Use Your Kinesthetic Child's Words
in Your Own Speech

Once you know the new words that your kinesthetic child is trying to learn, look for opportunities to use them in your speech when your child is around. See if your child recognizes the word and what you mean in your usage of the word. Have bonus words for the day. Tell your child that you are going to use some of the new vocabulary words and to keep his or her ears open for them. You can also have the child use new words in his or her own speech.

Give your child a bonus point leading to a tangible reward for noticing that you used the new word or for times when your child used the new word in his or her own speech. For each word used in speech, award one point and a bonus point for each successful sports move, whether basketball, golf, football, or soccer. These can add up to prizes your teen would enjoy winning.

Your child will appreciate the interest you are taking in his or her vocabulary work. At heart, children love the attention they receive from parents as you take the time to help them improve in the various skills.

Kinesthetic Prize Chart

Directions: Parents can work with their child or teen to decide the number of points to earn doing the activities in this book needed to earn prizes. Decide on smaller prizes, medium size prizes, and larger prizes for which the points can be exchanged. (You can make up your own list of points. Below is an example.)

Number of Points	Prizes
50 points	_____
100 points	_____
250 points	_____
500 points	_____
750 points	_____
1000 points	_____
2000 points	_____

Points earned: Day 1____   Day 2____   Day 3____   Day 4____

Day 5____   Day 6____   Day 7____   Day 8____   Day 9____

Day 10___   Day 11___   Day 12___   Day 13___   Day 14___

Day 15___   Day 16___   Day 17___   Day 18___   Day 19___

Day 20___   Day 21___   Day 22___   Day 23___   Day 24___

Day 25___   Day 26___   Day 27___

Total points:_____

About the Author, Ricki Linksman

Ricki Linksman, author of *How to Learn Anything Quickly* (Barnes and Noble publishers), and *Solving Your Child's Reading Problems, The Fine Line between ADHD, ADD, and Kinesthetic Learners: 197 Kinesthetic Activities to Quickly Improve Reading, Memory, and Learning: The Ultimate Parent Handbook for ADHD, ADD, and Kinesthetic Learners*, and over a dozen books on brain-based accelerated learning, is one of the nationally recognized accelerated learning experts. Ricki has developed a simple Internet assessment called "Superlinks to Accelerated Learning™" (www.superlinkslearning.com) to help anyone find his or her fastest way of learning and the best strategies to use for accelerating learning and improved communication.

For students, the Superlinks methodology is available to improve reading, study skills, and test-taking skills (for grades pre-K, K-12, and college) in an online program accessible to parents and teachers called Keys to Reading Success®" (www.keystoreadingsuccess.com). This award-winning program has raised 88-99% of all students (K-12 and college) from 2-5 grade levels in reading in 4 to 6 months. Ricki has been honored by the IASCD WINN research award for raising reading levels in a public school in less than a school year. Her proven techniques has raised ISAT (state reading test) scores and California state reading test scores in public schools that were not meeting state standards to meeting and exceeding state standards, in less than a school year. Her success in raising reading scores quickly includes both inner city and suburban schools, public, private, and charter schools, including regular education, gifted, special education, Title 1, ELL (English language learners), bilingual, honors, and those students with ADD or ADHD or dyslexia. She uses accelerated learning techniques to train parents and teachers quickly so they can use her assessments, tools, and strategies to bring rapid results to students.

As founder of National Reading Diagnostics Institute and Keys Learning, headquartered in Naperville, Illinois, she offers reading diagnostic testing, Superlinks assessments, and one of the most results-driven, proven accelerated tutoring and test prep in the world today to raise performance of students within weeks and months—not years. She offers training to parents and teachers in her methods so they can help students accelerate learning and raise reading achievement, scores, and grades in the shortest possible time (www.readinginstruction.com).

Ricki hosts frequent webinars, phone seminars (teleseminars) and trainings for parents and teachers and schools on accelerating learning for children and adults of all ages and all learning styles (visual, auditory, tactile, and kinesthetic, both left brain and right brain hemispheric preferences) to help each person achieve their highest potential and fulfill their dreams of success.

For trainings for parents and teachers, visit: www.readinginstruction.com
For information, contact National Reading Diagnostics Institute and Keys Learning.
Email: info@keyslearning.com
For other product, books, audios, coaching, and summer or after-school courses produced by Ricki Linksman visit any of the following: **www.readinginstruction.com**
www.keystolearningsuccess.com   **www.keyslearning.com**
www.keystoreadingsuccess.com   **www.superlinkslearning.com**

Other Resources Available from Ricki Linksman

For other product, books, eBooks, audios, videos, coaching, and summer or after-school courses produced by Ricki Linksman visit any of the following:

The Fine Line between ADHD or ADD and Kinesthetic Learners: 197 Kinesthetic Activities to Quickly Improve Reading, Memory and Learning in Just 10 Weeks: The Ultimate Parent Handbook for ADHD, ADD, and Kinesthetic Learners, by Ricki Linksman
(To order, visit: **www.keystolearningsuccess.com/FineLineADHD**

Off the Wall Phonics: For Kids on the Move): Kinesthetic Phonics Games: (10 Award-winning Game levels of 10 games each to accelerate reading. Prove to raise reading levels in 98% of all students (grades K-12) by accelerating them from 3-5 grade levels through these 10 game levels. (To order, visit: **www.offthewallphonics.com/OrderSpecialAll**

Keys to Reading Success™: An online Internet based pre-K-12 and College accelerated brain-based reading program, with reading diagnostic tests, phonics diagnostic tests that parents or teachers can use and a Superlinks assessment to find students' fastest way of learning, including learning style and brain hemispheric preference; an individual prescriptive plan on improving reading, and thousands of lesson plans and fun activities from pre-K-12, and college in all components of reading (comprehension, phonics, fluency, vocabulary, test-taking skills, memory, and phonemic awareness) in all learning styles (visual, auditory, tactile, and kinesthetic) (The phonics test and Superlinks test is available in Spanish also) \
Visit: www.keystoreadingsuccess.com

Superlinks to Accelerated Learning™: An online Internet brain-based assessment to find one's fastest way of learning, including learning style and brain hemispheric preference; and a detailed individual report with strategies on best way to learn, best materials to use, and best way to communicate (pre-K, K-12, college and adult) (Spanish version is also available).
Visit: www.superlinkslearning.com

For other product, books, audios, coaching, and summer or after-school courses produced by Ricki Linksman visit any of the following:
www.readinginstruction.com   **www.keystolearningsuccess.com**
www.keyslearning.com   **www.keystoreadingsuccess.com**
www.superlinkslearning.com

Kinesthetic Vocabulary Activities Your Child Will Love: In Just 27 Days Improve Your Kinesthetic Child's Vocabulary and Reading Comprehension

by Ricki Linksman
(Author of *How to Learn Anything Quickly and The Fine Line between ADHD* and *Kinesthetic Learning: 197 Kinesthetic Activities to Quickly Improve Reading, Memory, and Learning: The Ultimate Parent Handbook for ADHD, ADD, and Kinesthetic Learners*) Published by National Reading Diagnostics Institute)

Kinesthetic Vocabulary Activities Your Child Will Love: In Just 27 Days Improve Your Kinesthetic Child's Vocabulary and Reading Comprehension can help end your frustration as a parent. It provides answers to the burning questions tens of thousands of parents and teachers of kinesthetic children have asked me, including: How do I develop my kinesthetic child's vocabulary when he or she cannot sit still and thinks vocabulary is boring?

Kinesthetic learners learn vocabulary using different strategies and activities from learners of other learning styles such as visual learners, auditory learners, or tactile learners. Students with a right-brain preference learn differently from those with a left-brain preference. If traditional methods of learning vocabulary words are not working for your kinesthetic child, it could be that the teaching method does not match your kinesthetic child's method of learning.

If you are looking for fun, engaging kinesthetic vocabulary activities for a kinesthetic learner of any age from pre-school, pre-K, or grades K-12, or college or adult, then this book will provide you activities that I have found make a difference in only 27 days. These kinesthetic vocabulary lessons and activities can accelerate and improve your child's vocabulary and reading comprehension. I have tested and proven these activities to work with tens of thousands of children of all ages around the world. These activities will engage your kinesthetic child of any age (pre-K-12) in fun activities while improving vocabulary and raising reading comprehension.

Why wait for an important test, a state reading test, or the ACT or SAT college prep tests to try to cram thousands of words into your kinesthetic child's brain in a few weeks? Start today and give your child the competitive edge to have great reading comprehension and a great vocabulary to succeed in any content area subject, reading, or in tests.

ISBN: 978-1-928997-17-7
National Reading Diagnostics Institute